DATING FOR TEENS

DATING FOR TEENS

JUDE HAWTHORNE

CONTENTS

1 Introduction   1

2 Understanding Teen Dating   3

3 Communication Skills   5

4 Building Trust and Respect   7

5 Setting Boundaries   9

6 Dealing with Conflict   11

7 Digital Etiquette and Online Relationships   13

8 Self-Care and Mental Health   15

9 Healthy Sexuality   17

10 Dating Violence and Abuse   19

11 Peer Pressure and Influence   21

12 LGBTQ+ Relationships   23

13 Dating and Social Media   25

14 Cultural and Religious Perspectives on Dating   27

15 Building Confidence and Self-Esteem   29

16 Balancing School and Relationships   31

17 Support Systems and Seeking Help   33

18 Parent-Teen Relationships and Communication   35

19 Long-Distance Relationships   37

20 Ending Relationships Respectfully   39

21 Moving On and Self-Reflection   41

22 Resources and Further Reading   43

CHAPTER 1

Introduction

Our handbook will help all of us learn how to build strong and healthy relationships. We decided to make it after speaking with the students in our senior English class who said they did not feel prepared for dating relationships. Even though all of us know healthy relationships are very important for teens, many of us do not know how to build a strong dating relationship that will last. They shared stories about times when they wished they knew how to handle dating situations, and we realized that our teachers and parents had not talked to any of us about dating. We agreed that being educated about dating would help us build healthy relationships, so we wrote this for you and for us. Keep in mind that we are teens, so our handbook may not include all the dating dos and don'ts, but it can help all of us to start building strong and healthy dating relationships.

We are starting by looking at the benefits of dating. Then we will dive into how to build a strong dating relationship by first getting to know yourself. We will explore who you are, your interests, and your values. We will take time to build a safe dating network. After all, the people close to you can help guide you through your dating relationship. We also will take time to talk about obstacles to dating. All of us may fear getting hurt or getting pressure for sex, but there are ways of dealing with those dating realities and more. Finally, we will explore different dating relationships: casual dates, exclusive dating, or just hanging out. Each type can help you get great dating experiences.

CHAPTER 2

Understanding Teen Dating

Dating is an important activity that helps teenagers learn more about themselves and other people and helps them to establish themselves as separate from their parents and other family members. Generally, romantic relationships develop slowly over time. Teenagers who grow up in loving, caring families learn how to be good friends and eventually romantics, which is a valuable skill that they can always use. Many teenagers have friends who are boyfriends or girlfriends. Dating today can be very different from when you were young. Sometimes one boy or girl can feel so opposite from themselves in terms of values and goals that they can feel alone and out of place. Social situations like school, play, work, church, clubs, and other activities can provide opportunities to ask and accept dates.

Human behavior is a combination of how they think, feel, and act. Feelings are the foundation of all of this. Relationships are an important context and opportunity for interpersonal growth that includes feelings and learning to master them. This includes understanding one's own feelings, understanding the feelings of others, and learning skills to express complex emotions in healthy ways. Relationships with family, friends, and romantic partners all provide opportunities for this type of growth. According to experts, knowing how to attach to others is one of the signs of emotional growth in teenagers. In addition to increasing parental and peer relationships, the romantic component of adolescence is associated with important developmental tasks such as the development of autonomy. For example, being in a secret romantic relationship may indeed be a sign that a person has separated his or her romantic life from his or her parents.

CHAPTER 3

Communication Skills

Communication plays a critical role in our relationships. The way we send and receive messages and the way we interact around our communication has a direct effect on the health and strength of our connections with others. To build positive relationships and deal with conflict in safe and effective ways, it is important to develop and practice your communication skills. This section highlights the kinds of communication skills that are healthy for dating and other kinds of close relationships.

Some of the essential communication skills for healthy relationships include the following:

Active listening: One way to demonstrate to your partner, date, or friend that you care about what is important to them is to let them know that they are being heard. Active listening is a good way to do this.

Effective expression of feelings: Telling others how we feel can sometimes be challenging. Being able to express positive feelings such as love and joy as well as "problem feelings" such as anger, hurt, or fear becomes important in our close relationships.

Open and honest communication: Speak truthfully and to the point. Don't be afraid to ask for clarification if you are not sure you understand or if something appears to be left out. If you mess up, apologize or do your best to right that wrong. Openness includes sometimes opening up your heart to feelings and experiences. You may want to share a last date or other good time you recently had to show that you are also open to developing a better connection.

CHAPTER 4

Building Trust and Respect

For your relationship to be healthy, you need to trust the person you're with and feel that person respects you. Here are some examples of trust and respect. When we built this list, you said these are the qualities you most want to have in your relationship. Trust can be built in many ways. It starts with honesty. You both need to practice honesty and reliability for trust to grow. Spend time together, learn to communicate well, listen and respond to what the person says. If the person reacts badly when you tell him or her the truth, it may indicate that the person is not ready for a close relationship. Let this relationship unfold naturally. Open yourself when it seems right, and let the other person open when that seems right.

It feels good when people say "Thank you," or "Please," or "You are welcome." We build self-respect by respecting others and by knowing that we are valuable. Respect can be shown in many ways. Keep to the rules. When you say you will do something, do it. Make decisions together. Ask your friend what they would like to do and make a compromise. Good IQ (intelligence), good behavior, and a positive attitude are three tips for showing respect. When you feel respected, you also feel safe. When you feel safe, you feel peaceful and respected. Be committed to yourself, as well as anyone you invite into it. Have self-respect. Have respect for the person you're inviting into your life. The more committed you are to yourself, the more capacity you have to build a committed relationship.

CHAPTER 5

Setting Boundaries

What are boundaries? What do they have to do with dating? And what does it mean to be "boundary-crossed"? In the context of healthy and unhealthy relationships, the establishment and respect of boundaries are incredibly important aspects to consider. Chances are you aren't dating someone who has the same exact boundaries or comfort levels (and that's ok, because we are all different people!). To this end, we have to communicate with each other to come to an understanding of what is acceptable and unacceptable in a relationship.

Our boundaries might not be the same as our partner's boundaries, and that's okay. What matters is that both people are willing to respect each other's boundaries and be patient as each person decides what they are comfortable with. Similarly, a boundary could be crossed intentionally (such as pressuring someone even after boundaries have been established) or unintentionally ("We must have sex if you love me," or assuming your partner is comfortable with something because they haven't told you they're not). Learning to recognize and respect boundaries is a crucial part of a healthy relationship. Below are the dating contents relating to the theme of boundaries.

Content - Boundaries Reflect Respect: Shaping and Protecting Your Relationship (Module 5) - Establishing and Communicating

Boundaries: Shaping and Protecting Your Relationship (Module 4) - Right or Ratchet? (Lesson 1) - Talking about Boundaries (Lesson 3) - Are the Red Flags? (Lesson 3)

CHAPTER 6

Dealing with Conflict

Conflict is a normal part of any relationship, so it should come as no surprise that couples sometimes argue. This can be the result of many factors, including stress and miscommunication. Disagreements come up, and people need to recognize when they are needed and how to handle them when they occur.

Differing Perspectives: The fact that people are not the same makes disagreements quite inevitable. Two people who have lived entirely different lives are going to have different opinions. Recognize that just because someone has a different point of view does not mean that they are wrong. There are a number of ways to deal with conflict that will help bring the other person's point of view to light and help stop the arguing. Learn about some methods of constructive communication.

Identify the Cause: One of the best ways to reach a settlement when in disagreement is actually understanding what started the disagreement in the first place. Many people will disagree on an issue that has nothing to do with the real problem. Addressing the real issue can often help end the conflict.

CHAPTER 7

Digital Etiquette and Online Relationships

Going to the movies, watching a game, going for a bike ride, reading a book together, going for pizza after the game, dancing together in your room, meeting for dinner after going out with your friends, and talking on the phone can be considered dates. During a date, some teen couples talk about their future wedding, college, and moving in together. Whether you are just chatting or hooking up at your house, listening to music at a party, or sharing an online conversation, getting together is how you begin and maintain relationships with friends and boyfriends and girlfriends. More and more young couples are moving beyond just hanging out and becoming boyfriend and girlfriend through electronic means.

The number of teens who are staying in touch with their current boyfriend or girlfriend online is growing too. If you are going to have a long-term relationship, it will greatly impact your relationship, your friends, your study habits, grades, and exercise and sleep habits. This booklet is to help you conduct all digital interactions and develop successful boyfriend/girlfriend relationships. With the digital world around us, many teen relationships start online. Most first-time interactions with someone new, a boyfriend or girlfriend, or a friend will be in a digital environment. After meeting someone online, it is best to meet face-to-face in a mutual, public location while with a friend or adult. While relationships of every kind must be built on a strong level of respect, trust, honesty, commitment, and shared hope for the future, creating an online connection can be challenging. To expand that digital relationship to a face-to-face world, safely yet openly and honestly.

CHAPTER 8

Self-Care and Mental Health

How teens take care of their emotional self and mental health is an integral part of what it means to be motivated, healthy, and fulfilled as a teen. In this section, the reader is taught about the value and importance of self-care. Additionally, teens who read this section develop an appreciation for and understanding of mental health, possibly even noting a few things that they can do to help improve their mental health. A self-assessment quiz or check-off will likely be included. If they feel concerned about friends, the readers are informed on how and why they should seek help. Minors may not engage in the course of conduct. Teens who have these concerns will gain an understanding about the emotional and mental range of healthy adolescents, be aware of acceptable ways to make oneself feel better or feel good and understand that it is possible to improve one's mental health. Also, readers and participants will understand the signs of a mental health problem or issue, and that it is important to ask for and receive support from appropriate sources.

The second half of this handbook prepares readers for a set of topics that are presented in ten subsequent lessons. Teens learn the importance of taking care of their emotional self as they grow, learn, and mature into motivated, productive, healthy and happy students and adults. The section is designed to introduce students to the concept of mental health and methods for good mental health. After teens read and apply the information presented in this section, they will be able to: explain the importance of self-care and its place in living a healthy lifestyle, identify everyday activities that one can do to take care of one's self mentally, spiritually, and physically, list things that can be done to take care of yourself physically, and identify people or groups that can help when you feel upset, angry, or very stressed.

CHAPTER 9

Healthy Sexuality

Consent. A sexual relationship should be between two people who want it to happen. Just because someone is in a relationship with or has been sexually active with someone in the past does not mean you have the right to assume someone wants to have sex with you. Also, be sure your partner knows that if either of you is not ready or willing to have sex, that's totally okay. It is not okay to be pressured or guilted into any sexual activity. Communication is important, so you should be able to talk honestly and openly about what you both are ready for. Everyone has the right to say "no" to any unwanted touch or any activities they are not comfortable with without fearing the loss of a relationship, your friends, or the other person's opinion of you. This could involve anything from holding hands to hugging to kissing to fondling to intercourse.

Reproductive Health. Just as important as emotional readiness is the physical readiness to have sex. Do not have sex if you think you might not be ready for the possible outcomes. If you are sexually active, realize that many people do not want to discuss sex, but it is very important for a healthy relationship. If you or your partner (however unlikely) become pregnant, this could drastically change your life. Make sure you and your partner would be able to manage the outcomes of a sexual relationship. The only 100% way to avoid

STDs and pregnancy is by not having sex. However, sexuality curricula taught in this area teach some students that the only way to 100% avoid STDs is through refraining from any physical contact with anyone else.

CHAPTER 10

Dating Violence and Abuse

Dating for Teens: A Handbook for Building Strong and Healthy Relationships. Center for Disease Control and Prevention, 2020. Content created by Crystal Otts at Swanson High School.

Dating Violence and Abuse According to the US government, dating violence and abuse are behaviors being done by a "partner in a relationship to control the other partner. Partners may be married or not married; heterosexual, gay, or lesbian; living together, separated or dating". Dating violence and abuse happens at any age, including when someone is a teen. Like sexual violence, there are different types of dating violence, including physical violence, sexual violence, psychological aggression, and stalking. Eighty-one percent of parents believe teen dating is not an important issue. Because of these statistics and a perception of unimportance, 25% of parents have not talked to their children about domestic violence. In most cases, the abuse or violence is being committed by a girlfriend or boyfriend, but a small percent has been done by another. Abuse is not only being able to inflict physical harm on a partner, but the history shows an equal amount of partner violence done by girls on boys that is abusive or violent.

Do you know the signs of an abusive relationship? Different types of abuse include: • Physical: Hitting, slapping, breaking things, hitting or kicking walls • Sexual: Participating in unwanted sex, causing pain during sex • Emotional: Put downs, isolation, humiliation, intimidation • Financial: Withholding money, stealing money • Credit: WhenIHaveDaughter • Digital: Controlling an e-mail or social site log-in, monitoring calls or use of a cell phone • Stalking: Obsessive surveillance and pursuit, whether at school or electronically

How can you help if you think someone you know is in an abusive relationship? Talk privately to that person. Let them know you are concerned and that you are there for them. Offer advice and assistance in locating resources. Learn what help is available at your school and in your community. Lastly, organize a campaign to educate others - teenagers and adults - about the importance of recognizing and promoting healthy dating.

CHAPTER 11

Peer Pressure and Influence

The opinion of friends and close family has always been important to teenagers. As they enter their teenage years, peers develop an even greater importance. The influence of peers appears to be at its highest point in the teen years and diminishes as the individual moves into their 20s. Because peers are so significant in a teenager's life, some have said that adolescents are not sufficiently mature or individualized enough for a dating relationship. It is simply believed that they are following the tastes of peers rather than initiating and maintaining relationships for themselves.

At times, the influences are exerted subtly and not through direct suggestions. This makes it easy for a person to fall into dating activities. These pressures can affect individual thoughts, actions, and problem-solving abilities. But is peer influence bad? No. Influences can be good or bad. Some friends can negatively pressure you into dating or taking a risky relationship or situation. Others can positively pressure you into making good use of your time, talents, skills, and good use of relationships. Perhaps the most underscored substance of these influences is the power and flexibility of individual values. Your values should be the directive for your decision making.

As such, you are capable of making your own choices and decisions that show your values and guide your friendships and relationships. Only when one's values become weak in your mind can the grip of peer pressure become overbearing. Truly maintaining your values will help substantially dissuade against negative pressures. Some of the powerful values that you can focus upon that help steer one away from negative peer pressure include (but are not limited to) self-respect, considerate and responsible actions, problem-solving ethics, internal strength, ethical daily decisions, appropriate humor, and the right to be treated fairly at all times.

CHAPTER 12

LGBTQ+ Relationships

According to research, about 2-4% of people are gay or lesbian. What that means is that for every 100 teens, between 2 and 4 of them might be gay or lesbian. Additionally, about 2-3% of people are bisexual. For these reasons and many more, it is important that people talk about LGBTQ. What does that stand for? It means Lesbian, Gay, Bisexual, Transgender, and Queer or Questioning. Someone who is "queer" is still figuring out ways to describe their sexual orientation and/or gender.

Handling problems in a gay/lesbian/bisexual (GLB) relationship is a lot like dealing with common problems in a straight relationship. There may be other issues as well. Homophobia is fear and hatred of gay people. If your relationship needs help, look for adults or friends who accept you for who you are and do not believe in homophobic attitudes. It's important to find a safe place to talk with others about your relationship if you need help sorting things out. Most people base friendships and intimate relationships on shared learning and experiences. When one partner is less experienced sexually, it can make it more difficult (but not impossible) to share sexual feelings with the partner who is less experienced. This is why, especially if you are just coming out or if you are just starting a relationship, it is especially important to look for someone who will support and respect your feelings about keeping the relationship healthy without sex until you say it is time. Be cautious about moving too fast sexually. Rushing into sex before either partner is ready can undermine a new and promising relationship. In the same manner, every person is unique, every relationship is unique. Because of such sexual uniqueness, contraception and other pregnancy prevention methods must be used consistently and correctly.

CHAPTER 13

Dating and Social Media

Social media shapes how we interact and build our relationships. Because our romantic relationships are an important part of our lives, it makes sense that dating and social media are so intertwined. Surveys show that all age groups in the U.S. use social media platforms to reach out to those they are romantically interested in – including about half of 13- to 17-year-olds. Maybe this is because social media allows us to connect with others in fun, exciting ways. In fact, research suggests that a lot of the nice things people do in offline dating are done even more often in the world of social media. For example, people use social media to connect with others that share their interests and passions. Others show romantic links by labeling someone as boyfriend or girlfriend. Some people post pictures in album photos of them with their partners. They might also include comments or captions. For 13- to 17-year-olds, about 20% include comments with their pictures.

Good and Bad of Using Social Media to Connect When you use social media to explore dating, the information in the profile of your potential partner can give you a lot of information about his or her likes, dislikes, hobbies, aspirations, and common interests. The profile will tell you more about a person than you might gather from a few minutes of back and forth conversation in person. But some people try to make their friends jealous by using the internet to show off about their lives and boast. The amount of correspondence, attention, and value that someone gets from people who view and respond to his/her profile can become important to someone's identity. Let's think about Facebook. If someone is not asked to become "friends," or is asked and the other person is handling privacy settings and "unfriend you," getting a reputation as a friend-worthy friend is well-liked and respectable. If you post on another person's wall and get no responses back, this may be seen as ignoring your message, unimportant, or even rejected for asking you to say something controversial or negative. Some people may say that they "defriend" because someone is too dramatic in their profile, sharing too much or being inappropriate – calling it "Facebook etiquette."

CHAPTER 14

Cultural and Religious Perspectives on Dating

Societies and cultures around the world show great diversity in their views of love and relationships. Understanding how such beliefs influence the individuals and families from these cultural backgrounds can help you serve them more effectively. My own work in this area has been primarily focused on Hispanics. Aspects of that work are woven through the topics in this handbook.

There is a great range of dating behaviors between cultures in the world, and even between subpopulations within the US. Several groups in the US place an especially high value on friendships and dating relationships. Amish and Mennonite young people are taught the value of working through relationships in their adolescent years, often in the activities of community clubs, and are encouraged in dating by the time they reach their mid-teens. Early friendships between Hasidic Jewish classmates can evolve into dating relationships that prepare the young person for the time when they become "marriage-minded." A few fundamentalist Christian teenage girls who participate in purity balls where they renounce premarital sex and promise to save themselves for their future husbands begin learning about relationships as they approach their sweet 16. Other groups in the US place little, if any, emphasis on friendships and relationships between young people. Among Muslims connected with the Islamic Center of Johnstown, dating is not viewed as a normative behavior. These young people go mostly to all-girl or all-boy schools, and they are not to develop romantic relationships until they are college-aged.

CHAPTER 15

Building Confidence and Self-Esteem

When we like ourselves, we will encourage others to like us too. So how do we become confident and like ourselves? Only you can answer that for yourself, but sometimes we can get help from friends and adults in speaking up and sharing what is wonderful and unique about us.

There are many things that can help individuals build their confidence and self-esteem. Some ways teens have told me they do this include spending time on things they are good at, honing a skill (like playing an instrument), helping others out, and contributing somewhere in their community. Most youth emphasize the importance of getting involved in hobbies, activities, and/or sports that interest you and make you feel good about yourself. It's also important to take time to acknowledge our positive traits and all the good things in our lives, rather than just focusing on the negative. Some dating survivalists suggest keeping a list of what attracts someone to us that can be looked at whenever we're feeling down. Focusing on the positive aspects of ourselves and nourishing our confidence through the use of positive affirmations has been found countless times to be a useful way to win over negative expectations.

CHAPTER 16

Balancing School and Relationships

Where do relationships fit in with my other priorities, such as school and sports?

Balancing school and relationships can be challenging. You already have a responsibility to do what you need to do for school and any other activities you are involved in. You can't eat, breathe, or sleep with another person in the same way you can with other parts of your life. Relationships are as important, but not more important, than other responsibilities. They often take a different kind of time than those other responsibilities—time in the afternoon or evening instead of time before or after school time or work time. Realizing that time with your boyfriend or girlfriend has a different place in your life is crucial.

Ideas for Working Both School and Relationship Responsibilities: - Set priorities. Determine what has to be done and then decide on the focus required for each. It is difficult to concentrate on schoolwork when your mind is on the person you are dating or vice versa. - Set aside time for both school and your relationship. A rule of thumb that should be followed is if you feel "smooshed" for time—do your schoolwork. Be sure that your social time is a time you can afford to use. - Let your boyfriend or girlfriend know when you are going to be busy with school. If you're working on a home-work assignment, let your boyfriend or girlfriend know that you have a specific amount of work to get done. Then, as soon as you get finished, let them know that you can talk or get together.

Support Systems and Seeking Help

Having a strong support system and knowing where to seek help are important skills for anyone, particularly for teenagers. Think about where you can go if you need support. You need a group of people you can turn to when you need help with something that is bothering you. It can be hard to admit it if you are feeling overwhelmed in a relationship, but there are people available to help. Looking for help does not make it seem like you are less of a person, but rather it shows you are using the support available to you.

Who Can Help? Here are a few people who may be able to help you in a difficult situation: family members, trusted adults, community programs, and technology. Knowing trusted adults is important. This can be anyone: extended family, teachers, counselors, school nurses or doctors, church leader, social worker, youth group leader, or police. It doesn't have to be just one person but can be a group of people. Many communities and schools have programs based on treating others with respect: LEAD, student council, peer counseling, file of life, Boys' and Girls' clubs. Technology can also be an option to gain support: Kids Help Phone, Ask an Expert - Kids

Help Phone, bullying.org, Virtual Big Brother, Virtual Big Sister, or children involved with CAS. Running away never solves the problem. Let someone help you keep the situation a safe one. Refusing help often does not get rid of the problem—it just extends it! Only when a person can observe and understand both nonverbal and verbal signals can they offer proper help as well.

Parent-Teen Relationships and Communication

Adolescents and their parents have started to prepare to move from the 'parent-child' relationship to a more adult, friend-like relationship. As you have entered the early dating scene, the relationships you have with your parents might have started to change as well. You will want to move beyond being treated as a little child with few rights or with an inability to think for yourself. You will want to be more independent, including the right to establish new friends and acquaintances. Your parents have a legal responsibility to take care of you and make sure you are safe and healthy. Parents are also concerned about protecting you from the possibility of being harmed in any way, including dating violence. One of the most important things that teens and parents, or any two people, can do is to keep lines of communication open. Many parents are open to their teenagers developing friendships as long as they have a relationship based on open and honest communication. Here are some tips for building a healthy and trusting relationship between teenagers and their parents.

Learn to see the situation from their point of view and to understand what they really mean to say. For example, if they say "We respect your right to make your personal choices," they want you to understand that they grant you more privileges and freedoms. On the contrary, if they say that they want you to get home by 11.30, they really expect you home by 11.30. Stay calm. Don't run to the phone to call your fellow date as soon as you get off the phone with your parents. If they are overly excited, they are likely to be less likely to protect you. Avoid fighting (getting into lengthy arguments) with your parents. Hug and kiss your parents hello and goodbye. They enjoy it, you need it too, and it creates happiness all around.

Long-Distance Relationships

Remote can still be real.

For all those dating through tech, long-distance can take a whole different form. Even though they are often just as meaningful, there are some big differences to keep in mind for LDRs (long-distance relationships).

Communication: No matter how you chat, texts and video calls can never be a replacement for spending time together in person. And just like talking to anyone, communication can feel messy when it's all words without facial expressions, body language, and other non-verbal cues. Expect misunderstandings, and do your best to use lots of kind words to help smooth them over.

Trusting: Let's be honest - online, people can be and do a lot of different things. It's important to go into any long-distance (and close-distance) relationship with trust and a positive attitude, but your long-distance relationship will be that much more awesome and joyful when you are able to fully trust each other. Create respectful ground rules together, like how often you can talk to other people, and make sure you always take their feelings, wants, and needs into account. Get their input along with their permission.

Talking and Connecting Beyond a Screen: Just like everyone should in a relationship, it's key to figure out how to really connect and bond, no matter whether or not you're near each other physically. This can mean a little bit of extra time talking about hopes, dreams, family, friends, books, or feelings, just to stay caught up and really feeling close.

CHAPTER 20

Ending Relationships Respectfully

Healthy relationships are filled with fun and laughter, but it also takes work. If a relationship isn't working, or it is turning unhealthy in some way, it can be important to end it. That can feel really tough, especially if the person looking to end things is worried about hurting the other person. Whether it is usually fun, the other person's partner reveals a different side, that decision and feelings are not respected, or that the negatives are outweighing the relationships, it can be hard to recognize. Ending a relationship is a skill and can be difficult to do, but it is important to be able to recognize when it is time to let go of the relationship itself.

Sometimes, a relationship doesn't feel right anymore because a person has grown apart from someone or because a crush has developed for someone different. When the relationship is not working and not respectful, it is time to end it before more harm is done. It may be difficult for the other partner to accept the breakup, and the hurt feelings may not go away quickly, but it is the right thing to do. Take care of oneself by talking to an adult and ending the relationships. It is most important to ensure regular safety and secure an exit plan before the breakup conversation. Be kind and respectful in a breakup conversation and think about carefully what the message will be. Speak kindly and make the other person's feelings as small as possible. Try and be fair in the future and continue to be respectful with the other person, despite the hurt feelings.

CHAPTER 21

Moving On and Self-Reflection

Some day you may want a different person in your life, and one who may be much more perfect for you. Breaking up with your boyfriend or girlfriend is a way to meet new people. When a relationship ends, it may be difficult; there may be many feelings of depression, disappointment, sadness, or anger. You can survive anything that might happen today and nothing is so bad that it could never happen again in your world. Surround yourself with a friend who cares about you personally. Somebody's so friendly when you're down helps a lot.

Afterwards, it's a healthy, thriving new partnership you're in and you've grown through that separation. And some day, from feeling like you've got your heart ripped out to taking a great relationship with someone else, you could. You have a chance to investigate yourself and expand after a break-up. Think about why your relationship ended. Even for your ex-boyfriend or girlfriend, remember, know how much stuff wasn't going right. You could create a quiz to refer to by jotting down your thoughts. What traits are you needing in a boyfriend or girlfriend for a successful future relationship? You see a much better picture of what you are looking for and pursuing in a healthy friendship when you take the time to think about these issues. It's really part of growing up to experience a breakup - not a chapter that causes rejection or individual embarrassment. A strong relationship demonstrates growing and getting resilience.

CHAPTER 22

Resources and Further Reading

For information and support in building healthy relationships, visit the following websites:

- ReachOut.com - aims to improve the mental health and well-being of young people so they can take advantage of life's opportunities - eFriends Toolkit - Building safe, supportive and respectful e-communities

If there are particular topics you would like to know more about, or if you were unable to complete any of the journal activities, these resources have been suggested to help support your continued learning in relationship education. All online material and links are current as of September 2005.

Journaling and Self-Reflection: - Taking Charge: an e-journal for young women - Self-Help on the Web - one woman's search for the perfect support site - One Look Can Change the Relationship - Relationship eJournals

Fostering Couple Relationships: - Fostering Healthy Couple Relationships

Gender Roles: - Tuff Chicks

Preventing Dating Violence: - Safe Dates - Mentors In Violence Prevention (MVP) Program - National Dating Abuse Helpline

Building Positive Peer Networks: - Positive Peer Culture - The Program for the Education and Enrichment of Relational Skills

Living Together: - Cohabitation in Australia - The Steps to a Successful Remarriage

The Life Cycle of Relationships: - The Couple Check-Up

Finding Your "Mr. Right": - Dating Revolution

"Hot" Relationships: - Keeping the "Heat" in Your Relationship - Keeping the Spark Alive

Addiction/Substances: - Love may not be all you need - Faces of speed

Surviving a Break-up: - Overcome Relationship Break-ups including Divorce and separation, Mental Illness, Drug addiction, the death of loved ones and more doesn't have to be that hard... it's an amazing place to start.